Noah's Ark

RETOLD BY
MARY PACKARD

ILLUSTRATED BY
DOREEN GAY-KASSEL

 A Golden Book • New York

Golden Books Publishing Company, Inc., Racine, Wisconsin 53404

A long time ago God was sad to see
Just how wicked people could be.

All but one man had lost their way.
Only Noah remembered to pray.
God was angry but then He knew
Exactly what He had to do.

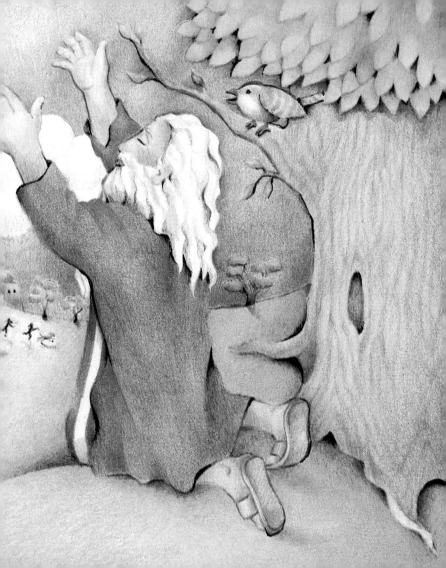

He would send a flood to wash away
The people who had gone astray.
All but Noah would lose their lives—
All but Noah, his sons, and their wives.

Rain clouds appeared. The sky grew dark.
God told Noah to build an ark:
"Fill it with beasts, both large and small—
Make the ark big to hold them all."

The raindrops fell, and strong winds blew.
The animals boarded, two by two:

Two of each kind—female and male—
From the tall giraffe to the tiny snail!

Lumbering beasts and leaping gazelles
Followed turtles with shiny shells.

With a bleat, a grunt, a screech, or a bark,
Each beast found a place upon the ark.

For forty days the rain came down—
It fell on every city and town.
The ark was tossed both far and wide.
"God will protect us!" Noah cried.

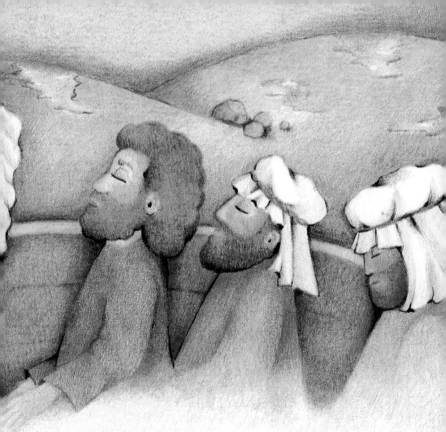

Then all at once the rain was through.
The sun came out—the sky turned blue.
The waters slowly went away,
And Noah's family knelt to pray.

The land turned green—the danger had passed.
It was time to leave the ark at last.
God promised Noah there and then
He would never send a great flood again.

God made a rainbow as a token—
To show His promise would never be broken.